# Remembering Armageddon:

## Reflections on a Century of War

*R. Bedford Watkins*

by R. Bedford Watkins

A LittleLeaf Press, Inc. PUBLICATION

Cover Image: The City of Sedan, France in Flames.
Photo Courtesy The World War II Preservation Society.

**Remembering Armageddon: Reflections on a Century of War.** ©2000, R. Bedford Watkins. First Edition. Printed and bound in the United States of America. All rights reserved.
ISBN 1-893385-03-5
LCCN: 99-067383

Published by Little Leaf Press, Inc., P.O. Box 187, Milaca, MN, USA 56353. Toll Free 877-548-2431. Fax (320) 556-3585. e-mail: littleleaf@maxminn.com
http://www.maxminn.com/littleleaf

**Publisher's Cataloging In Publication**
*(Provided by Quality Books, Inc.)*

Watkins, R. Bedford
    Remembering Armageddon : relfections on a
century of war / by R. Bedford Watkins. -- 1st ed.
    p. cm.
    LCCN: 99-67383
    ISBN: 1-893385-03-5

    1. World War, 1939-45--Poetry.  2. World War,
1914-18--Poetry.  3. War poetry, American.
I. Title.

PS3573.A8444R46 2000          811'.54
                    QBI99-1576

# for my sons

Robert Bedford Watkins, III
and
The Reverend Thomas Wyatt Watkins
in gratitude

for their love and encouragement
in the writing of these poems.

# contents

Soldiers of the 55th Armored Infantry Battalion and tank of the
22nd Tank Battalion move through smoke filled street. Wernberg,
Germany. Pvt. Joseph Scrippens, April 22, 1945. The National
Archives and Records Administration, Still Picture Branch (NNSP),
The Army Signal Corps, Record Group 111-SC-205298.

My subject is War, and the pity of War.
The poetry is in the pity.

*Wilfred Owen*

Cpl. R. Bedford Watkins, gunner, 515th Field Artillery Battalion, 7th Army, European Theater of Operations

# introduction

War brutalizes every life it touches, ennobling
some, anointing others with the seal of sacrifice,
sometimes destroying the ones who cannot suffer
the savagery.

Among those who survive, some share their story
with former comrades or understanding friends.
Others never speak of it. A few live every day
with the horror indelibly etched on the inner eye
of memory.

These poems reflect the sadness, the pathos, and
the often sardonic humor of men in battle. They
also express my rage at the maddening obscenity
of war as I remember my own experiences while
serving in the European Theater of Operations
during World War II. It is my hope that they may
resonate with others who were there.

R. Bedford Watkins

On the duckboards. World War I. Identifying a fallen comrade, Chateau Wood. Photograph courtesy of the Imperial War Museum, London.

# 1 At the Somme

This field is rife with flowers now,

more fertile than when weary men

in muddy puttees paced the slimy duckboards

tracing endless trenches lined with wire

and laced with hate, the haunting stench of war.

There gaunt men crouched in fear or dread,

or leaned a cautious head against

the sodden, sandbagged walls

to peer across the savaged land

where dead still lay,

or maybe to hear soft sobs of wounded,

still untended,

weeping in their lonely dying,

lying where they fell that summer day.

■ ■ ■

Deep below this blossomed earth

their bleak bones lie in silent, mirthless shade.

Forgotten now the hellish din

of screaming shell and spinning spray of shrapnel

in the deadly fire that fell from those indifferent skies.

For with them lies no calm repose,

no grace to face the requisites of death.

Gone is their principled conceit,

their firm defiance in defeat,

even their sweet life-giving breath.


■ ■ ■

The mawkish, unconsoling choir

of praise for noble sacrifice,

each tiresome phrase of tribute or remorse

lies hushed upon their bloody bier,

now buried in the near oblivion of the dreary sod.

Nor can a mem'ried smile be raised

except in grief

by those who loved them

and who gave them over to their glory

and to God.

July 16, 1916. 1st Battalion, Lancashire Fusiliers. The Fusiliers fix bayonets as they prepare to go "over the top" outside Beaumont Hamel in the Battle of the Somme. World War I. Photograph courtesy of the Imperial War Museum, London.

# 2 Rue Bordieu, 1917

Souls desolate and torn with dread—

    far worse than fetid shrapnel wounds

    or strands of shredded flesh—

wrench instant bravery from the ubiquitous,

    obscene dead,

rise dutifully from the filth of the intestinal trenches

and rush, mindlessly, into the raw, black maw of Hell.


Even Ares wept as legions fell facing full

    the devastating shell that swept clean

    every shattered feature above ground.

Again and then again, they ran at each command,

    enriching every bloody ditch they fell in.

Some lived and soon were moved to other fields,

    as brash, unwary pawns for further play.

■ ■ ■

They're coming now along a Caesar's road,

the way of warriors since before Augustus' day.

All night slow, lumbering caissons scar the ancient stones

and the narrow straat intones

a constant drum of endless ranks of weary men,

thoughtless but for the next stop nearer rest.


Rifle laden, rain sodden.

plodding in arrhythmic cadence,

thinking only of a sleep,

they trudge the muddy miles that take them,

guileless, to their final rest at Ypres.

The French march into captivity at Sedan. World War I, 1917. Captured German Photograph. Courtesy World War II Preservation Society.

July 1, 1916. World War I. Evacuating an early casualty.
Photograph courtesy of the Imperial War Museum, London.

# 3 Uncle Mack

Sitting beneath the summer trees,

his knobby knees drawn up to rest

his arms and mercifully ease

his trembling hands against his chest;

the grasping hands that had tried to press

the mask against his face as best

he could before he gasped and gagged

and sucked the fire into his breast.

Those hands that through long years practiced

no art nor plied a craft or threw

a ball to a son but only knew

the empty pain of sacrifice.

■ ■ ■

Sometimes at noon he'd tilt his face

to the burning summer sun and through

closed eyes he'd see the hellish place

he left his youth in the bloody dew.


Those restless hands that shook a ceaseless

rhythm through the years are blest

in stillness now, a hallowed peace

to sanctify a hero's rest.

"Then came the big day when we marched into Germany--right through the Siegfried Line." 1945. Courtesy The National Archives and Records Administration, Still Picture Branch (NNSP), Record Group 208-YE-193.

The USS Arizona burning after the Japanese attack on Pearl Harbor, December 7, 1941. Courtesy The National Archives and Records Administration, Still Picture Branch (NNSP), The Department of The Navy Record Group 80-G-32420.

# 4 Gene Hardin

Gently, still, the undulating surface swells to neap

and slowly falls in an eternal rhythm where you sleep

within the steel-hulled shell.

Nor can the solemn bell buoy

be heard within that hall of

honored dead entombed with all

their undone dreams forever resting in the deep.


We mourned you on that day, Gene,

we suppliants, as you lay

caught in the twisted bowels of the Arizona's gray

and shattered hulk. The waves

still wash the hold and lave

with love the white bones that still lie

just as you fell that winter "day of infamy"

in an inferno half a world away.            ■ ■ ■

And when men pray each year

      above your broken, briny bed,

what can they say about your sacrifice

that's not been said

      in studied, morbid prose

      or poetry by those

      of us who can never know

      your horror when you died below—

No matter, for our eloquence is lost among the dead.

The battleship USS Arizona (BB 39) underway in the 1930's. Official U.S. Navy photograph. Courtesy JCardin@aol.com. http://www.militarycity.com.

Pfc. Mickey Rooney imitates some Hollywood actors for an audience of Infantrymen of the 44th Division. Rooney is a member of a three-man unit making a jeep tour to entertain the troops. T5c. Louis Weintraub, Kist, Germany, April 13, 1945. Photo Courtesy National Archives and Record Administration, Still Picture Branch (NNSP), Army Signal Corps Record Group, 111-SC-203412.

# 5 U.S.O.

Stumbling through the old cobbled road

    into the dark street,

    listening for the sweet slurring of

    a blue-blared horn,

    the slight stirring of the heart

    at a familiar tune—

        no sound but the weary feet

        of a late night clerk,

        the harried cadence echoing

        along the damp, dreary

            corridor of vacant shops.

            (-- only a few more days

            before we move--)

■ ■ ■

From shadowed doorways come soft, lewd whispers,

an occasional intimate touch,

the artless offer of a crude caress

and promise of such a lust

as must be had to fill the emptiness—

no light but the waving wands

of search lights

near the ack-ack batteries

conducting their nightly symphony,

silently sweeping the corners

of the black abyss,

yellow brushes swaying over

praying hands and sleeping

children.

(--the channel can be rough

this time of year--)　　■ ■ ■

Just ahead a small band sound,

    rude siren with a mocking moan,

    luring lonely souls to the only sentient rock around.

    Passing through the black-out curtain

    into a bright revelry of tinseled solicitude,

    welcomed by a gracious, graying mother

    of a lost son—somewhere in the North Sea—

    offering the ubiquitous coffee and doughnuts

    with a sad smile and questions about

    home and family—

        a sharing of worn photos,

            of a young sister,

            a brave mother's face,

            the hometown football team —

■ ■ ■

an introduction to a young girl,

guileless in her faint perfume

and earnestness to please—her father

did not return from Dunkirk—

the warm, consenting flesh of her small hand,

the first cautious moves on

the barren warehouse dance-floor,

the unbearable sweetness of a girl in your arms

swaying to the cumbrous playing

of a valiant piano and a stodgy clarinet.

                    (--this may be the last time--)

■ ■ ■

Blinking lights signal the last dance.

 Polite goodbyes, well wishes,

 "God keep you safe."


Out into the night.

 An icy mist informs the many shining shapes

 that grace the gloomy street.


 Head down, collar up,

 return to base.

D-Day and Western Europe campaign, 1944-45. D-Day overhead aerial view, June 6, 1944. Normandy Beaches in an overhead aerial reconnaissance photograph. Men and assault vehicles storm the beaches, as wave after wave of landing craft unload their cargo, men move forward and vehicles surge up the roads. Courtesy U.S. Army Military History Institute. Official U.S. Army photograph number 51581.

# 6 Saar Basin: 1945

From the black spleen of holy-centered night

    and the fetid dank of our own

    dark days mourned,

    as the unseasoned borealis

    rumbled on the low horizon,

            the command came.


Slowly, a monstrous tube cranked skyward

elevating its obscene host,

    poised to spew the consecrated wafer

    into soft mouths screaming the ritual.

■ ■ ■

On the flank a tracered needlepoint swept cleanly,

    paused,

    and methodically resumed its stuttering stitch,

    sealing the seam of that

    particular patch of hell.

          The pause–the dreaded silence–then

the sky split, the crack peeled the

black skin of night raw-red,

shrill hell burst wide and spilled its excrement

across the damned,

squirming mole–like in holes,

their terror tearing through numbered

                    limbs

stretched on the leaden rack of fear.

■ ■ ■

Remembering the catechism

recalls the sense of doom

    of days we bled and gagged

    on the acrid stench of powder

    still burning memory's tongue;

    a comrade's scream still ringing,

    caught in the siren-filled,

    eternal din of our inhumanity.


    Hear the unconscionable benediction:

Be consoled. Dying finds its sweet mint

in the tightened grasp,

the heaving gasp of terror

melting instantaneously

on the shattered tongue of silence.

# 7 Alone

Alone,


lying mud-cushioned in a shallow shell hole,

    warmed only by the cold steel of my rifle,

as human marker for my unit to advance

    toward my position near the front,

I watch the wretched carnival

    and its various attractions

    curtained by the black night's chaos.


Just ahead arrhythmic staccato cracks

of small-arms fire

    punctuate the deep-dinning artillery—

a demonic music drowning the hilarious screams

    of desperate actors playing their life away.

■ ■ ■

A machine-gun's rapid snare

splits the crude cacophony

    and an occasional cymbal clash of lead shot

careens off a steel fire shield.


On the low horizon Ares paints fiery, red swatches

    like a gaudy sideshow canvas,

an ever-changing, kaleidoscopic caricature

of death as art.


The entertainment continues

    as the acrid stench of powder

permeates the low-lying mist

    like remembered popcorn.

■ ■ ■

Soon we'll enter stage left

    to join the glorious maelstrom

and taste again the insatiable rage of war.


    Suddenly,


a shocking silence ends the action.

    No applause is heard—

only the intense straining to hear

    the slightest sound of any movement.


I lie motionless in chilling sweat,

    staring into the ominous, black abyss,

        alone.

A lanky GI, with hands clasped behind his head, leads a file of American prisoners marching along a road somewhere on the western front. Germans captured these American soldiers during the surprise enemy drive into Allied positions. Captured German photograph. December, 1944. Photo Courtesy The National Archives and Records Administration, Still Picture Branch (NNSP), Army Signal Corps Record Group 111-SC-198240.

Moving up through Prato, Italy, men of the 370th Infantry Regiment, have yet to climb the mountain which lies ahead. Bull, April 9, 1945. Courtesy The National Archives and Records Administration, Still Picture Branch (NNSP), The Army Signal Corps Group 111-SC-205289.

# 8 The Helmet

Moving up slowly

       through the thin, dirty snow

       that covered ruined rows

       stapled by winter stubble

       to the unyielding field,

            we paused,

       wary of the ill-concealed rubble

       from a recent fight

       still strewn across the ravaged ground.

■ ■ ■

Coast Guardsman Charles Tyner, Fireman first class, examines the jagged shrapnel hole in the helmet he wore during the initial assault on the beaches of Southern France. Tyner suffered just a superficial scratch. Photo Courtesy The National Archives and Records Administration, Still Picture Branch (NNSP), The Coast Guard Record Group 26-G-2748.

To the right

    a single helmet,

    like a fat tortoise, lay alone,

    one clean hole through the center

    of the forehead,

    a few bone splinters,

    a little flesh, still fresh,

    pinned beneath the edge,

        an unintended monument –

            probably bobby-trapped –

        a modest stela

        commemorating one sudden rise to glory.

■ ■ ■

Always a surprise,

    death in war

    leaves little time

    to savor the sacrifice—

        an instant explosion of blinding light,

        the abrupt dark of nothingness,

        ----------------------------illimitable silence.

Marine Pfc. Douglas Lightheart (right) cradles his 30-caliber machine gun in his lap, while he and his buddy Pfc. Gerald Churchby take time out for a cigarette, while mopping up the enemy on Peleliu Island. Cpl. H. H. Clements, September 14, 1944. Courtesy The National Archives and Records Administration, Still Picture Branch (NNSP), The Marine Corps Record Group 127-N-97628.

# 9 "After a fire-fight..."

After a fire fight,

after the wounded, whimpering or screaming

or stoically staunching the urge to cry,

have been taken to the rear,

after the dead have been moved,

an unholy calm comes,

broken only by the occasional harassing fire

of a 105

or the whispered offer of a cigarette.

■ ■ ■

No birds sing,

the holes of small creatures are deserted,

a soft-soughing wind may move the oily smoke

rising from a shattered vehicle

or brush a lonely stalk of weed.

The stillness, like a mantle of peace,

lies over the carnage.


Exhausted, men recover from the terror slowly,

check their ammo, shift the dirt in their holes

for a more comfortable lie


                       and wait.


■ ■ ■

As the evening damp descends

their fear-fed sweat begins to chill.

Darkness invites the welcome warmth

in the glow of a cigarette

underneath a tented blanket

and a K-ration with tepid canteen water.


Taking hand grenades and extra ammo

they crawl to a hurried briefing for a night patrol,

and, soon after, move out.

American Generals:
seated left to right are
William H. Simpson,
George S. Patton, Jr.,
Carl Spaatz,
Dwight D. Eisenhower,
Omar Bradley,
Courtney H. Hodges, and
Leonard T. Gerow;
standing are
Ralph F. Stearley,
Hoyt S. Vandenberg,
Walter Bedell Smith,
Otto P. Weyland, and
Richard E. Nugent.
Circa 1945. Courtesy
The National Archives and
Records Administration,
Still Picture Branch (NNSP),
Record Group 208-YE-182.

American Troops of the 28th Infantry Division march down the Champs Elysee, Paris, France, in the "Victory Parade." Poinsett, August 29, 1944. Courtesy The National Archives and Records Administration, Still Picture Branch (NNSP), The Army Signal Corps Record Group, 111-SC-193197.

American soldiers, stripped of all equipment, lie dead, face down in the slush of a crossroads somewhere on the western front. Captured German photograph. Belgium, ca. December 1944. Courtesy The National Archives and Records Administration, Still Picture Branch (NNSP). Army Signal Corps Record Group 111-SC-198245.

# 10 Two Beneath a Tree

They lay as if asleep —

the head of the younger on the shoulder of the older

like a brother.

A light frost glistened

on the stubble of a graying beard

and sealed a stale saliva bubble

playing on pale, lifeless lips.

■ ■ ■

Swaying in a soft, Schwarzwalder breeze

the indifferent trees in tidy rows

spread a green pine panoply

above their untroubled rest.

Dressed in woodsman's clothes

and cobbled boots, their visage showed

no hint of horror to suggest death's throes,

no wounds or signs of grief in either face,

no evidence, no trace of fear

in their repose.

■ ■ ■

Since the fighting was so near

we could not pause to hear

the eloquence of their silent peace

but moved steadily windward

toward the clear, sharp sounds of war.

Nor could we comprehend

the twisted warp of fate

that left two innocents

as weft in death's design.


In war, men must leave enigmas such as these

behind them.

Perhaps a sorrowing wife or mother

soon might find them.

July 26, 1944. A member of a battery of 155mm field artillery units is putting a shell in the chamber in preparation for firing on the German lines in France. Official U.S. Army Photograph. Courtesy U.S. Army Military History Institute. Photo No. 191992.

Mammoth 274mm railroad gun captured in the U.S. Seventh Army advance near Rentwertshausen easily holds these 22 men lined up on the barrel. Although of an 1887 French design, the gun packs a powerful wallop. Courtesy The National Archives and Records Administration, Still Picture Branch, photo number NWDNS-111-SC-203308.

# 11 "Sorry, I just cannot..."

"Sorry, I just cannot become ecstatic

over the new ones – the M16, multiple

warheads, etc. Give me the old crossbow,

or better yet, the saber. Now there's

a weapon you can make a part of you—

you can feel the cleave and puncture

much like a strong trout on a flyline.

Some people are a little squeamish about it.

They prefer it neat and clean, push-buttony,

but that way you tend to lose the sport in it,

the glory, too.

■ ■ ■

Even women are protesting these days,

asserting their right to be heard, in tears—

"Do not weep, maiden," the poet said.

Hell, women always weep,

but you can make them forget—

there are ways!


Yeah, war's too impersonal these days.

I miss the closeness, the him-or-me gamble,

that one-on-one contact, which, after all,

is the basis for the best in human relationships.


I remember the second day after we were committed,

we were moving slowly through this small wood......."

Nurses of a field hospital who arrived in France (via England and Egypt) after three years service. Parker, August 12, 1944. Photo Courtesy The National Archives and Records Administration, Still Picture Branch (NNSP), Record Group 112-SGA-44-10842.

General of Cavalry von Kleist. Note the K on the fender of
the staff car. Captured German photograph. Photo Courtesy
World War II Preservation Society.

# 12 The Enemy

The shattered 88 listed to the right in the gun

emplacement. The shell holes near the site revealed

the deadly devastation of our fire.


One was left behind.

He lay half in the sun

in full uniform and helmet

and with a stunned look in glazed, half-closed eyes,

the half-surprise that death in war can bring.

His face betrayed how he had tried to cling to life

and wondered why I had not died instead of him,

or why his fire had been less true.

■ ■ ■

The grim reality we knew—

circumstance determines fate;

the whim of chance,

the dance of unknowns

circling 'round our centered core

that cautioned us to wait for want of knowing

if his fire would be more lethal than before.


Had he, too, friends, a lover,

dreams of wise ways to discover

deeper hues of happiness?

■ ■ ■

Could I have loved him as a brother,

though an enemy, an other than my kind

I had to kill?


Perhaps in still another place

we'll touch, embrace, and there

we can remember without rancor

that our own much-bloodied inhumanity's design

through given grace, was made divine.

July 28, 1944. While the ruined town is still being shelled by German tanks and artillery, this tired Yank infantryman takes himself a well-earned nap in Marigny, France. Official U.S. Army Photograph. Courtesy U.S. Army Military History Institute, Photo No. 192004.

# 13 Dooley

Dooley was an artist. One

whose cursing was so deftly done

that none could match his wanton wit

or even catch a hint of his despair.


His canvas was the air he breathed,

his tongue a brush that seethed with filthy

epithets and crudities

that gushed in endless, carping repartee.


His art of scathing diatribe

on everything that fueled his vile

irreverence could bring a smile

even from those who sought to squelch

his sordid prose.

■ ■ ■

Once caught straddling a slit trench

when a barrage came he hit

the putrid pit full face down

and lay throughout the twenty rounds

then rose in stinking rage to spit

obscenities beyond the bounds

of even man's depravity.


In exquisite detail he cursed

the Huns who crewed the guns describing

their bestial provenance—their kin

and forbears all had been of such

unspeakable birth that purest evil

could not bring its Mephistophelian

force to sting their tail but could only

fling them below the lowest ring of hell.    ■ ■ ■

He'd curse in verse and, even worse,

elaborate upon a word

that never could be heard again

untainted as it once had been.


Sometimes his blasphemies could be construed

as near approaching prayer, a rude

beseeching for a grace to hold

the fiendish joy that lit

his vivid face.

■ ■ ■

And later, after he was shot

and sent back to the rear, we got

no word of what he said, except

that when the night was clear

and the front was still

it was said by some that they could hear

a faint, familiar profanity

that lay like a low, thin mist

around our battered hill.

And some of those who heard then thought that

somewhere, maybe a world apart,

Dooley was still practicing his art.

August 16, 1944. Saint Maxime Area, France. Paratroopers of the 463rd Paratroop Field Artillery arrive in Saint Maxime. They are the first to get back to the beach area after their jump. They met little resistance. Official Army Photograph. Courtesy U.S. Army Military History Institute, Photo No. 377607.

Standing in the grassy sod bordering row upon row of white crosses in an American cemetery, two dungaree-clad Coast Guardsmen pay silent homage to the memory of a fellow Coast Guardsman who lost his life in action in the Ryukyu Islands. Benrud. ca 1945. Courtesy The National Archives and Records Administration, Still Picture Branch (NNSP), Coast Guard Record Group 26-G-4739.

# 14 "Grieve the fallen..."

Grieve the fallen in a thousand fields

> now lying in shallow, sunken graves

> or rotting beside a withered copse,

> their riotous worms working a wondrous way

> of fetid richness.


Praise the chosen underneath

> the town square monument bearing his name

> and extolling his deeds of killing.


Heed the passing bells that toll

> the exceeding sadness

> for the dead and those who mourn them.


■ ■ ■

Listen to the lame litany

in the hush of death and

hope of resurrection.


Preach the glory of battle

to young, eager minds

that they may also thirst

for the slaughter and the sacrifice.


■ ■ ■

Hail humanity's progress

    toward the perfection

    of insensate, obscene cruelty.


        In the name of holy WAR,


            Amen

Liberty Party. Liberty section personnel aboard LCM returning to USS Casablanca from Rara Island, off Pitylieu Island, Manus. PhoM1c. R. W. Mowday, Admirality Islands, April 19, 1945. Courtesy The National Archives and Records Administration, Still Picture Branch (NNSP). Department of The Navy Record Group 80-CASA-618.

# 15 War Museum

Crawling along with the slow-moving crowd,

the boy and his father viewed with much interest

the many artifacts in the vast exhibit hall.

Huge machines, many stories high, of all sizes,

shapes and designs. Some with wheels, others with

tracks. Almost all had hollow tubes of various sizes

protruding at different angles and seemingly

sophisticated guidance and operating systems.

A few had what appeared to be some kind of wings

as if they were meant to fly, but the boy couldn't

believe that the heavy, inflexible wing material

could actually lift such a monstrous mechanism

into the air.

■ ■ ■

What brilliant minds, what intelligent beings

to conceive and build such gigantic devices,

he thought.

The boy stopped at one curious display.

It seemed to be made of a substance similar to

the bones of large, dead animals he had seen.

It was long—seven or eight times as long

as the boy himself—slightly curved and knobby.

■ ■ ■

With his father looking over his shoulder

the young cockroach read the tablet:


– – – – – BELIEVED TO BE THE LEFT METATARSAL

OF A ONCE NUMEROUS AND THRIVING

CREATURE BELONGING TO A SPECIES OF

HOMINOID, NOW EXTINCT.

Crossed rifles in the sand are a comrade's tribute to this American soldier who sprang ashore from a landing barge and died at the barricades of Western Europe. 1944. Courtesy The National Archives and Records Administration, Still Picture Branch (NNSP). The Coast Guard Record Group 26-G-2397.

# 16 "Lay him gently..."

Lay him gently underneath the tree.

Cover what's left of his face.

He was proud of his neat mustache—

      his girl friend used to trim it for him—

      he said she liked to feel it on her face

      when she kissed him.

Why didn't he keep his head down?

What was he looking for?

■ ■ ■

He had planned to marry

    and open a small printing shop—

    he was good with machinery.

Wash the blood off the dog-tags—they'll

    send those home.

What size combat boots do you wear?

    These are almost new.

Check his billfold to be sure there's nothing

    he wouldn't want his mother to see.

    Graves Registration is not always careful.

    <u>DIVE!</u>        <u>INCOMING!</u>

With a canvas tarpaulin for a church and packing crates for an altar, a Navy chaplain holds mass for Marines at Saipan. The service was held in memory of brave buddies who lost their lives in the initial landings. Sgt. Steele, June, 1944. Courtesy The National Archives and Records Administration, Still Picture Branch (NNSP). The Marine Corps Record Group 127-N-82262.

# 17 "Bedcheck Charlie"

Old Charlie came around each night,

buzzing, diving, dipping right above our guns,

tipping his wings to see the dark ground

for any sign of light that might be left uncovered.


He hovered over each new-found thatch,

searching each low-crowned hummock

then sputtered away to another, further field

or black-edged patch and fluttered briefly,

lurching like a comic, mustachioed Munchhausen.


The risky game was played as well

with ack-ack on a nearby hill

which finally found his range

and hit him with a twenty-millimeter shell.      ■ ■ ■

He fell a few feet from my hole.

We dragged him from the cockpit whole but shattered

like a thin, loose sack of broken coal.


And curious to see the comic face

imagined from our hidden place

we turned him roughly on his back.

The beardless skin was cleanly peeled

from below his chin to the top of his brow.

The bloody, frontal skull revealed

no humor there nor any trace

of amusement on his vacant face.

Chow is served to American Infantrymen on their way to La Roche, Belgium. 347th Infantry Regiment. Newhouse, January 13, 1945. Courtesy The National Archives and Records Administration, Still Picture Branch (NNSP), The Army Signal Corps Record Group 111-SC-198849.

Two anti-tank Infantrymen of the 101st Infantry Regiment, dash past a blazing German gasoline trailer in the square of Kronasch, Germany. T4c. W. J. Rothenberger, April 14, 1945. Courtesy The National Archives and Records Administration, Still Picture Branch (NNSP), The Army Signal Corps Record Group 111-SC-206235.

June 14, 1944. Gen. Dwight D. Eisenhower, Gen. Henry Arnold, Adm. Ernest King and Gen. George Marshall, top ranking officers in the European Theater of Operations, aboard a landing craft enroute to the coast of France to inspect American installations. Official U.S. Army photograph. Courtesy U.S. Army Military History Institute, Photo No. 191528.

Jewish civilians. Copy of a
Captured German photograph
taken during the destruction
of the Warsaw Ghetto, Poland,
1943. Courtesy The National
Archives and Records
Administration, Still Picture
Branch (NNSP), Record Group
238-NT-282.

A German girl is overcome as she walks past the exhumed bodies of some of the 800 slave workers murdered by SS guards near Namering, Germany. Bodies were laid here so that townspeople would view the work of their Nazi leaders. Cpl. Edward Belfer. May 17, 1945. Photo Courtesy The National Archives and Records Administration, Still Picture Branch (NNSP), Army Signal Corps Record Group 111-SC-264895.

# 18 "Do not dwell..."

Do not dwell on the carnage—

    the shredded tendrils of torn flesh,

    the lead embedded in a fresh wound,

    no trace of a missing head,

    but there, a fair, young face

    burned beyond recognition.


Pay no attention to the bare, rough-cut feet,

    the bloodied hands trying to stuff

    a sweet, severed gut back into

    the gaping, intestinal hole,

    an anguished soul reaching

    with one good hand

    for a shattered arm blown off,

    lying five feet away in the scattered debris,

    still gripping the loaded clip. ∎ ∎ ∎

Ignore the quizzical visage

of one sitting motionless beneath a tree,

a clean hole through his left eye

and the back of his head blown out.


Do not doubt the certainty that the quiet one,

now crazed with numbing, crippling fear,

will spend his friendless days

thumbing a blank page of memory

and then relive the horror each night

when, exhausted,

he can resist sleep no longer.


■ ■ ■

Men learn to kill and go to war for duty's sake

or even for a fancied thrill

or yearned-for sting of instant glory.

Those who return bring more

than just their own

compelling story—

the boding bell,

the whispered fear,

the thump of shell,

the shrill hell of a night barrage—

Some still wage their raging war in silent memory.

91

A truck load of bodies of prisoners of the Nazis, in the Buchenwald concentration camp at Weimar, Germany. The bodies were about to be disposed of by burning when the camp was captured by troops of the 3rd U.S. Army. Pfc. W. Chichersky, April 14, 1945. Courtesy The National Archives and Records Administration, Still Picture Branch (NNSP). The Army Signal Corps Record Group 111-SC-203464.

# 19 Landsberg, 1945

We entered the compound

through the barbed-wire gate, now open,

a short while after it had been abandoned.

Everything in the camp was bleak, colorless,

only black and dirty gray.

In the center of the muddy enclosure

were several hundred bodies,

piled like discarded wood

three to four feet high.

The dead who were clothed at all

wore the ubiquitous, filthy, pajama stripe,

no shoes, no coat.

■ ■ ■

Remembering, Lord,

the hatred,

the squalor,

the beatings,

the cold,

the misery of untold terror and pain,

O, the sufferings inflicted again and

again and again.

Who can forget?

Who then can forgive?

The wooden barracks, doors locked,

were set afire. Arms and hands, late writhing,

still extending from beneath the walls

■ ■ ■

where they had desperately clawed

the frozen soil of the dirt floor to get out

but could not escape the flames.

Remembering, Lord,

the hunger,

the torture,

the lack of water,

the sound of derisive laughter

and being spat upon,

the horror of seeing a loved one slain,

O, the inhumane brutality seen again and again

and again.

Who can forget?

Who then can forgive?

■ ■ ■

And in a nearby wood

a dozen or more bodies

machine-gunned to pieces,

a head here, an arm there,

like meat, torn apart and strewn about.

The only color,

the white, emaciated skin

on fleshless bones,

stark against the dark forest floor.


Remembering, Lord,

never a kind word,

never a smile,

only curses heard,

only the vile corrupting hatred                    ■ ■ ■

spilled on every vestige of

humanity that remained.

O, the profane bestiality borne again and again

and again.

Who can forget?

Who then can forgive?


Three young men somehow escaped the slaughter,

hiding in a small bunker atop a nearby hill.

We found them, pajama-clad, eyes glazed,

lips swollen, numb with hunger, cold and fear.

We gave them food and clothing.

I gave one my last two packs of cigarettes.

He lowered his bruised head

and with cracked lips

he kissed my hand.                              ■ ■ ■

O, the sufferings inflicted again and again

and again.

Remembering, Lord,

Your love for all,

even for these.

Through Your given grace,

perhaps one can forget,

perhaps even forgive.

Prisoners in the concentration camp at Sachsenhausen, Germany. December 19, 1938. Photo Courtesy National Archives and Records Administration, Still Picture Branch (NNSP). Record Group 242-HLB-3609-25.

# 20 The Wall

. . . WALTER PRITCHARD . . . ALTON WILLIAMS, III . . .

. . . THOMAS F. DORAN . . .

        chiseled in black granite,

        reflected in the faces

        of those who read the names.

. . . SAMUEL I. KEMP . . . HAROLD ARNOLD . . .

. . . BILLY RAY MOORE . . .

        names of the fallen – fathers, sons, lovers —

        whose fair flesh fed the ravenous maw

        of war's obscenity.

■ ■ ■

Dedicated to Major David W. Schilling, USAF Ret.
Copyright by David Schilling, Jr. Sgt. USAF 1971-75.

The long, black stela crypts

the brooding spirits of those honored dead

which hover over all who stand

in sacramental silence to remember.


And when they touch a well-loved name

a healing comes, and peace,

like touching the garment of Christ.


■ ■ ■

. . . CHARLES T. MC CORKLE . . . JOSE LOPEZ . . .

. . . HARRY CURTIS MC CARTNEY. . .

. . . JAMES BAINES WOODS . . .

Children of an eastern suburb of London who have been made homeless by the random bombs of the Nazi night raiders, waiting outside the wreckage of what was their home. September 1940. Photo Courtesy National Archives and Records Administration, Still Picture Branch (NNSP). Record Group 306-NT-3163V.

# 21 "A day will come..."

A day will come

when silence drowns the battle's din

and men will creep from bunkers

deep within the ruined earth

to wring their wrath at what their hate has brought.


And when the long-sought peace has come

some little child will smile

spilling a tearful mirth as rain,

filling our arid souls with joy

where pain had been.


■ ■ ■

Then weary men may sit beside

their humble door

in quietness,

remembering what they struggled for.

Their comrades lie in honor now

beneath a foreign cross,

reminder of the grievous loss they bore

and symbol of their sacred vow

that war will be no more.

2nd Lt. William Robertson and Lt. Alexander Sylvashko, Russian Army, shown in front of sign (East Meets West) symbolizing the historic meeting of the Russian and American Armies, near Torgau, Germany. Pfc. William E. Poulson, April 25, 1945. Photo Courtesy National Archives and Records Administration, Still Picture Branch (NNSP). Army Signal Corps Record Group 111-SC-205228.

# Appendix

■ ■ ■

The Author and the Publisher wish to gratefully acknowledge those men and women whose photographs grace these pages, and those organizations and government agencies, with whose permission we reprint them here.

Special thanks to...

The National Archives and Records

Administration, Still Picture Branch (NNSP),

The Army Signal Corps,

The Department of The Navy,

The Coast Guard,

The Marine Corps,

The Office of War Information,

The U.S. Army Military History Institute,

The World War II Preservation Society,

The Imperial War Museum, London.

and

David Schilling.

# Index To Images

112

Page 20
The USS Arizona burning after the Japanese attack on Pearl Harbor, December 7, 1941. Courtesy The National Archives and Records Administration, Still Picture Branch (NNSP), The Department of The Navy Record Group 80-G-32420.

Page 23
The battleship USS Arizona (BB 39) underway in the 1930's. Official U.S. Navy photograph. Courtesy JCardin@aol.com. http://www.militarycity.com.

Page 24
Pfc. Mickey Rooney imitates some Hollywood actors for an audience of Infantrymen of the 44th Division. Rooney is a member of a three-man unit making a jeep tour to entertain the troops. T5c. Louis Weintraub, Kist, Germany, April 13, 1945. Photo Courtesy National Archives and Record Administration, Still Picture Branch (NNSP), Army Signal Corps Record Group, 111-SC-203412.

Page 30
D-Day and Western Europe campaign, 1944-45. D-Day over-head aerial view, June 6, 1944. Normandy Beaches in an over-head aerial reconnaissance photograph. Men and assault vehi-cles storm the beaches, as wave after wave of landing craft unload their cargo, men move forward and vehicles surge up the roads. Courtesy U.S. Army Military History Institute. Official U.S. Army photograph number 51581.

Page 37
A lanky GI, with hands clasped behind his head, leads a file of American prisoners marching along a road somewhere on the western front. Germans captured these American soldiers during the surprise enemy drive into Allied positions. Captured German photograph. December, 1944. Photo Courtesy The National Archives and Records Administration, Still Picture Branch (NNSP), Army Signal Corps Record Group 111-SC-198240.

Page 38
Moving up through Prato, Italy, men of the 370th Infantry
Regiment, have yet to climb the mountain which lies ahead.
Bull, April 9, 1945. Courtesy The National Archives and Records
Administration, Still Picture Branch (NNSP), The Army Signal
Corps Group 111-SC-205289.

Page 41
Coast Guardsman Charles Tyner, Fireman first class, examines
the jagged shrapnel hole in the helmet he wore during the initial assault on the beaches of Southern France. Tyner suffered
just a superficial scratch. Photo Courtesy The National Archives
and Records Administration, Still Picture Branch (NNSP), The
Coast Guard Record Group 26-G-2748.

Page 44
Marine Pfc. Douglas Lightheart (right) cradles his 30-caliber
machine gun in his lap, while he and his buddy Pfc. Gerald
Churchby take time out for a cigarette, while mopping
up the enemy on Peleliu Island. Cpl. H. H. Clements,
September 14, 1944. Courtesy The National Archives and
Records Administration, Still Picture Branch (NNSP), The
Marine Corps Record Group 127-N-97628.

Page 48
American Generals: seated left to right are William H. Simpson,
George S. Patton, Jr., Carl Spaatz, Dwight D. Eisenhower, Omar
Bradley, Courtney H. Hodges, and Leonard T. Gerow; standing
are Ralph F. Stearley, Hoyt S. Vandenberg, Walter Bedell Smith,
Otto P. Weyland, and Richard E. Nugent. Circa 1945. Courtesy
The National Archives and Records Administration, Still Picture
Branch (NNSP), Record Group 208-YE-182.

Page 50
American Troops of the 28th Infantry Division march down the
Champs Elysee, Paris, France, in the "Victory Parade." Poinsett,
August 29, 1944. Courtesy The National Archives and Records
Administration, Still Picture Branch (NNSP), The Army Signal
Corps Record Group, 111-SC-193197.

Page 52
American soldiers, stripped of all equipment, lie dead,
face down in the slush of a crossroads somewhere on the
western front. Captured German photograph. Belgium,
ca. December 1944. Courtesy The National Archives and
Records Administration, Still Picture Branch (NNSP). Army
Signal Corps Record Group 111-SC-198245.

Page 56
July 26, 1944. A member of a battery of 155mm field artillery
units is putting a shell in the chamber in preparation for firing
on the German lines in France. Official U.S. Army Photograph.
Courtesy U.S. Army Military History Institute. Photo No.
191992.

Page 56
Mammoth 274mm railroad gun captured in the U.S. Seventh
Army advance near Rentwertshausen easily holds these 22 men
lined up on the barrel. Although of an 1887 French design, the
gun packs a powerful wallop. Courtesy The National Archives
and Records Administration, Still Picture Branch, photo number
NWDNS-111-SC-203308.

Page 59
Nurses of a field hospital who arrived in France (via England and Egypt) after three years service. Parker, August 12, 1944. Photo Courtesy The National Archives and Records Administration, Still Picture Branch (NNSP), Record Group 112-SGA-44-10842.

Page 60
General of Cavalry von Kleist. Note the K on the fender of the staff car. Captured German photograph. Photo Courtesy World War II Preservation Society.

Page 64
July 28, 1944. While the ruined town is still being shelled by German tanks and artillery, this tired Yank infantryman takes himself a well-earned nap in Marigny, France. Official U.S. Army Photograph. Courtesy U.S. Army Military History Institute, Photo No. 192004.

Page 69
August 16, 1944. Saint Maxime Area, France. Paratroopers of the 463rd Paratroop Field Artillery arrive in Saint Maxime. They are the first to get back to the beach area after their jump. They met little resistance. Official Army Photograph. Courtesy U.S. Army Military History Institute, Photo No. 377607.

Page 70
Standing in the grassy sod bordering row upon row of white crosses in an American cemetery, two dungaree-clad Coast Guardsmen pay silent homage to the memory of a fellow Coast Guardsman who lost his life in action in the Ryukyu Islands. Benrud. ca 1945. Courtesy The National Archives and Records Administration, Still Picture Branch (NNSP), Coast Guard Record Group 26-G-4739.

Page 74
Liberty Party. Liberty section personnel aboard LCM returning
to USS Casablanca from Rara Island, off Pitylieu Island, Manus.
PhoM1c. R. W. Mowday, Admirality Islands, April 19, 1945.
Courtesy The National Archives and Records Administration,
Still Picture Branch (NNSP). Department of The Navy Record
Group 80-CASA-618.

Page 78
Crossed rifles in the sand are a comrade's tribute to this
American soldier who sprang ashore from a landing barge and
died at the barricades of Western Europe. 1944. Courtesy The
National Archives and Records Administration, Still Picture
Branch (NNSP). The Coast Guard Record Group 26-G-2397.

Page 81
With a canvas tarpaulin for a church and packing crates for an
altar, a Navy chaplain holds mass for Marines at Saipan. The
service was held in memory of brave buddies who lost their
lives in the initial landings. Sgt. Steele, June, 1944. Courtesy
The National Archives and Records Administration, Still Picture
Branch (NNSP). The Marine Corps Record Group 127-N-82262.

Page 84
Chow is served to American Infantrymen on their way
to La Roche, Belgium. 347th Infantry Regiment. Newhouse,
January 13, 1945. Courtesy The National Archives and Records
Administration, Still Picture Branch (NNSP), The Army Signal
Corps Record Group 111-SC-198849.

**Page 85**
Two anti-tank Infantrymen of the 101st Infantry Regiment, dash past a blazing German gasoline trailer in the square of Kronasch, Germany. T4c. W. J. Rothenberger, April 14, 1945. Courtesy The National Archives and Records Administration, Still Picture Branch (NNSP), The Army Signal Corps Record Group 111-SC-206235.

**Page 85**
June 14, 1944. Gen. Dwight D. Eisenhower, Gen. Henry Arnold, Adm. Ernest King and Gen. George Marshall, top ranking officers in the European Theater of Operations, aboard a landing craft enroute to the coast of France to inspect American installations. Official U.S. Army photograph. Courtesy U.S. Army Military History Institute, Photo No. 191528.

**Page 86**
Jewish civilians. Copy of a Captured German photograph taken during the destruction of the Warsaw Ghetto, Poland, 1943. Courtesy The National Archives and Records Administration, Still Picture Branch (NNSP), Record Group 238-NT-282.

**Page 88**
A German girl is overcome as she walks past the exhumed bodies of some of the 800 slave workers murdered by SS guards near Namering, Germany. Bodies were laid here so that townspeople would view the work of their Nazi leaders. Cpl. Edward Belfer. May 17, 1945. Photo Courtesy The National Archives and Records Administration, Still Picture Branch (NNSP), Army Signal Corps Record Group 111-SC-264895.

Page 92
A truck load of bodies of prisoners of the Nazis, in the Buchenwald concentration camp at Weimar, Germany. The bodies were about to be disposed of by burning when the camp was captured by troops of the 3rd U.S. Army. Pfc. W. Chichersky, April 14, 1945. Courtesy The National Archives and Records Administration, Still Picture Branch (NNSP). The Army Signal Corps Record Group 111-SC-203464.

Page 99
Prisoners in the concentration camp at Sachsenhausen, Germany. December 19, 1938. Photo Courtesy National Archives and Records Administration, Still Picture Branch (NNSP). Record Group 242-HLB-3609-25.

Page 101
Dedicated to Major David W. Schilling, USAF Ret. Copyright by David Schilling, Jr. Sgt. USAF 1971-75.

Page 104
Children of an eastern suburb of London who have been made homeless by the random bombs of the Nazi night raiders, waiting outside the wreckage of what was their home. September 1940. Photo Courtesy National Archives and Records Administration, Still Picture Branch (NNSP). Record Group 306-NT-3163V.

Page 107
2nd Lt. William Robertson and Lt. Alexander Sylvashko, Russian Army, shown in front of sign (East Meets West) symbolizing the historic meeting of the Russian and American Armies, near Torgau, Germany. Pfc. William E. Poulson, April 25, 1945. Photo Courtesy National Archives and Records Administration, Still Picture Branch (NNSP). Army Signal Corps Record Group 111-SC-205228.

# About The Author

R. Bedford Watkins served in 1944 and 1945 as a gunner corporal, 515th Field Artillery Battalion under the 7th Army in the European Theater of Operations.

Sailing by convoy from Camp Kilmer, New Jersey, on October 30, 1944, his battalion arrived in Liverpool, England, and a few weeks later moved from a marshalling area across the English Channel to Le Harve, France, to Camp Twenty Grand, a staging area for combat preparation.

They were soon ordered to the front. Passing through the Maginot Line they began the push on the Saar Basin, moving and firing almost continuously. On March 27th the battalion crossed the Rhine River at Worms on a pontoon bridge and helped carry the offensive into the aggressor's own land, stopping only a few days before VE Day.

After the war he followed his passion earning a Bachelor of Music degree from Rhodes College, the Master of Music degree from the University of Michigan and the Ph.D. degree from the University of Iowa.

He taught at Rhodes College, Winthrop University and for 32 years was a member of the faculty of the School of Music at Illinois Wesleyan University, where he served as Chairman of the Keyboard Department.

While at Illinois Wesleyan he performed solo recitals on harpsichord and piano at colleges and universities in 25 eastern, southern and midwestern states.

He has composed and published works for instrumental solo, chamber music, orchestra, band, vocal solo, and choral music.

His poetry has received outstanding reviews and publication in IRIS, a journal of poetry and art, and Eternity Magazine, as well as two broadsides and two collections of poetry published by Pilot Rock Press.

Today, Dr. Watkins and his wife Eugenia are busy with retirement at their beachfront home in north Florida, staying in close touch with family and grandchildren, walking, running and performing for the joy of it.